POEMS FROM THE PRISON PLANET

by J. Martin Strangeweather

Cover artwork by J. Martin Strangeweather
Design by Dustin Myers
Published by the Santa Ana Literary Association
Santa Ana, CA 92701
Printed in the United States of America
ISBN 979-8-218-04862-4

this is dedicated to the countless victims

of discrimination & injustice

00001

I used to write love poems in barbwire.

But lately there's been too much politics
in my poetry.

On the upside,
there's been a glut of poetry
in my politics.

00002

Prisons are shortsighted.

Prisons foster hypocrisy, dishonesty, and cruelty,

both inside and outside their walls.

Prison bleeds into the mind,

and the imprisoned mind bleeds its prison mentality

into the streets,

then the neighborhoods,

then your kids.

Sometimes it will literally bleed out of their bodies.

00003

How can a mind that hasn't mastered itself

ever hope to master the minds of others?

Corruption in any prison system

starts with the prison authorities.

The good guys are always the bad guys, too.

Always.

The bad guys are just more honest

about their badness.

Prisoners need mentors and senseis,

not guards and wardens.

00004

Laws are based on

ever-shifting

social, psychological, and economic contexts.

Laws are ultimately arbitrary.

No laws are good laws.

Maybe we should do away with laws

and replace them with guidelines,

learning curves,

and psychosocial repercussions.

Social rehabilitation rather than institutionalization.

00005

Every law

has a police officer's club enforcing it.

Every law

is backed by a bullet.

Confucius viewed laws as harmful—

they never fix the source of criminal activity,

and often lead to more negative repercussions

for society as a whole.

Too many laws reduce morality

to a shameless act of evading punishment & justice.

Such a society is unable to foster ethical behavior,

only the fear of consequences.

A human will strain to be free

when they are severely restricted,

as any animal would.

00006

In matters of justice, Confucius says:
"Righteous examples of proper living
motivate ethical conduct better than
the threat of punishment."

Too many regulations actually dissolve the capacity
for ethical comprehension,
resulting in a society of unthinking automatons
bereft of morality beyond the rules
they are forced to obey.
An abundance of laws can only lead
to rampant dishonesty and hypocrisy.

Every new law indicates
a miscommunication of goals
between the government and its citizens.

The only way to reharmonize the masses

and reconcile them with their leadership

is for the politicians

to represent themselves through deeds

in a manner consistent with their words.

00007

Prisons are an indication of a nation's
morals and ideals.
Prisons are a reflection of society's shortcomings.
Prisons reveal a government's lack of imagination.

Prisons are a lifestyle.
Prison culture is a choice,
not an inevitability.

00008

Prisons teach citizens how to be criminals—

how to smuggle and sell drugs,

how to run the game.

Prisons teach criminals how to be gangsters.

Prisons teach gangsters how to be prisoners.

Prisons teach prisoners how to hate

and murder their fellow human

for no real reason.

Prisons condone criminality.

Prisons encourage criminality.

Prisons foster criminality.

Why?

Because prisons capitalize on criminality.

00009

Q: What must change before prisons can change?
A: Our priorities.

Where is punishment learned?
Where is learning rewarded?

Are you trying to punish the wrongdoers,
or rehabilitate them?

Prisons can teach citizens that they're criminals,
or teach health risks how to live healthier lives.

00010

Is criminal behavior a failure of society

or the individual?

Might it be both,

since the two are intimately connected?

Confucius says:

The role of a government is to provide

for the needs of its citizens

in three basic ways:

1) Provide sufficient resources

   for adequate living conditions.

2) Provide sufficient protection from enemies.

3) Provide the citizens with confidence

   that the first two needs

   are being provided for.

Above all,

a good system of governance

ensures the prosperity

of each and every citizen.

Most men steal and kill because of want.

What if we weren't always left wanting?

Everyone is afraid they don't or won't

have enough,

even if they already have too much.

The way things are nowadays,

you can never have enough.

Enough what?

Comfort?

Safety?

Love?

None of these can be assured,

but it would certainly help the state of things

if everyone were given a modest "existence wage"

in return for upholding the unwritten social contract.

Not exactly socialism,

not quite communism,

let's think of it as collective capitalism,

or contextual capitalism,

or reasonable capitalism,

or non-extinction capitalism,

or even compassionate capitalism.

The coffered dome ceiling of achievement

would still possess an oculus

open to the heavens of limitless potential,

but its light would not be screened

from shining upon us all.

00011

Make no mistake,

we are a collective consciousness, of sorts.

Consciousness is born from

the collective unconscious,

which arises from mutually shared external factors,

to say nothing of the role mass media

and advancements in telecommunication

have played

in the homogenization

of our psyches.

Materialist philosopher Thomas Hobbes claimed

all humans enter into an unwritten social contract

when they decide to occupy the same general area,

mutually agreeing

to give up certain (primal) freedoms

that are counterproductive

to a healthily functioning society.

Hobbes compared society to a body.

One could also compare the entire species

of *Homo sapiens*

to a single, group-minded body.

Just as the hands and feet must be subservient

to the will of the head,

so must the laborers and craftsmen obey

the dictates of their ruler(s).

Only when the desires of the masses

(the cells that make up the body politic)

and all the different factions and organizations

(the organs of the body politic)

are aligned with the will of the ruling class

(the brain of the body politic)

can the body politic function effectively.

Wherever such a synergistic society occurs,

it manifests as a god

with the power to transform the world,

or at least its local landscape.

The body politic scenario presupposes
effective leadership,
but right now we're in a body whose head
is governed by its stomach,
a body whose brain believes it is more important
than its fingers and toes.

What good is a brain without musculature,
or musculature without skeletal framework,
unless we're talking about worms?

The lifeblood of the body politic is money.
Blood needs to circulate freely
throughout the body politic
if we're to survive and live healthy.

no trillionaires

+

no billionaires

=

no poverty

(it's not that hard to figure out)

00013

Every nation on Earth
would have more than enough wealth
if we just abolished war,
along with the need for
billion-dollar defense budgets.

Hasn't the time come
for the war on war?

00014

Q: How could we ever get rid of war?
A: Level the playing field.

The world currently has
about 13,000 nuclear warheads.
What if we distributed those warheads equally
throughout every nation on Earth?
13,000 godly displays of might
divided by 195 nations
equals approximately 66 nukes per nation
(66.6 to be exact).

This is just one idea
among countless others.
I invite you
to come up with your own.

00015

So long as war is profitable,
there will be war.

So long as blood is appraised expendable,
good blood will go to waste.

Rule #1 for achieving world peace:
War must never be initiated;
weapons are for self-defense only.

Rule #2 for achieving world peace:
See rule #1.

Let acts of war be put to a vote,
decided by those who'll be
expected to do the fighting.

Conscript the politicians first,
conscript the bankers second,
and if they should all perish, well…

00016

If a world without war seems unrealistic
it's only because too many of our leaders are

slimy
yellow-bellied
worms

&

green-eyed
forked-tongue
snakes.

Cast your vote:

☐ bullheaded birdbrain

☐ pigheaded jackass

What can you do
when the animals run the zoo?

00017

Primary and secondary school shootings
in the U.S.
as of 5/24/2022:

Lindhurst High School: 4 dead, 10 injured
Cleveland Elementary School: 5 dead, 32 injured
Thurston High School: 4 dead, 23 injured
Westside Middle School: 5 dead, 10 injured
Columbine High School: 15 dead, 21 injured
Red Lake Senior High School: 10 dead, 7 injured
West Nickel Mines Amish School: 5 dead, 5 injured
Sandy Hook Elementary School: 28 dead, 2 injured
Marysville Pilchuck High School: 5 dead, 1 injured
Stoneman Douglas High School: 17 dead, 17 injured
Santa Fe High School: 10 dead, 14 injured
Oxford High School: 4 dead, 7 injured
Robb Elementary School: 21 dead, 15 injured

The saddest thing about this list

(which is by no means exhaustive)

is that by the time you read it,

I fear it will need to be updated.

There have been 27 school shootings in the U.S.

this year,

and the year isn't even halfway over.

Politics are bleeding from our sons and daughters.

When did we start

expecting schoolchildren

to be braver

than politicians?

00018

J. Martin Strangeweather read this "poem" at ten virtual open mic poetry readings across the U.S. during the month of November.

"Friends, frenemies, and haters alike, I stand here before you this evening as one of America's spoiled sons, stained with the guilty blood of seven generations. My trust in the United States government is at an all-time low, and I know I'm not alone. But what are we supposed to do? How do we curtail the growing incompetence and dishonesty rooted within the current two-party system? Throw away our vote on a third party? How's that going to help anything? How could we give a third party a truly relevant voice? What if we formed a political party with the specific intention of never getting anyone from our party elected? What if we formed a political party whose only goal was to tip the scales of the other two parties? Ladies and gentlemen, I present to you the Least Odious Party, or the L.O.P.s—the Lops, or even better, the Loppers, as in the party that lops off the head of would-be tyrants, a third party whose sole purpose is to cast their votes for the least odious candidates of the two major political parties in any given election. And how would we define the least odious candidates, you might be asking? Simple: those who are the least driven by greed, vanity, and prejudice. Our campaign slogan would be 'Vote for Compassion and Empathy!' Regardless of which candidates our constituents vote for, they will always be able to proclaim with confidence, 'I'm voting for the Least Odious Party!' This would be a third party where you'd never feel like you were wasting your vote. You would indeed be the ultimate swayer of every election, direct and impartial. The presence of the Least Odious Party would presumably have the effect of forcing the other two major parties to clean up their act, at least superficially. You have to start somewhere. Granted, there are a few kinks that need to be worked out, but I only have a three-minute time slot here to save the world. I'm not claiming this is *the* answer. It's just *an* answer, and a rather silly one at that. What I'm really saying is, the problems we're facing aren't insurmountable. We just have to start thinking more creatively, more boldly."

00019

Posted to Facebook on 6/15/2022:

Hey there, friends, frenemies, and curiosity seekers. I was selling poetry books at a music festival in downtown Santa Ana last Saturday, sharing a booth with a buddy of mine who restores and sells old typewriters, Abel Stearns. I asked everyone who stopped by our booth to finish this sentence: "A good leader…" But they had to type out their answer on one of Abel's restored typewriters. At the end of the day, I assembled their responses into a poetic statement on leadership. Most of the collaborative poem was written by the public, though I added a few peculiar lines of my own. I thought some of you might like to read it…

She asked if I was an alien.
I said, "What does it matter?"
She said, "It doesn't. So, does that mean you're
an alien?"

A good leader
cares more about future reconciliations
than past grudges.

Nowadays, Jesus' twelve disciples
would have been nine Judas'
and three Doubting Thomas'.

Bravery on the battlefield is overrated.
I'd vote for peacetime empathy
if it were ever on the ballot.

Strength of character
over strength of arms.

A good leader
is never in it for money, fame,
or honor.

A good leader
is more concerned about homelessness and injustice
than their legacy.

A good leader
helps others grow,
but knows when to get out of the way.

A good leader
knows weeds & wildflowers
play an important role in nature.

A good leader
respects everyone as equals,
including their enemies.
*(those who believe otherwise
are not fit to lead)*

Nowadays, Buddha's ten disciples
would have been seven undercover CIA agents
and three KGB.

We're all in this fight together,
unless what you're really fighting for
is the supremacy of your ego.

And let's face it,
that's what most of our world leaders
are fighting for.

Death never comes to conquer.
Death is only a guide.

She asked if I believe
aliens were living among us in disguise.
I said, "I believe there are beings among us
who are masquerading as humans."

A good leader
seeks not to lead,
but to follow.
(those who do not grasp this
should not be leaders)

A good leader
speaks their mind to your face,
not behind your back.

A good leader
is never jealous
of other people's success.

A good leader
measures their success
by the prosperity of everyone they lead.

A good leader
learns from their mistakes
and the mistakes of others.

A good leader
uses their words to nourish and heal,
not to poison ears and fan the flames.

A good leader
understands how all threatening words
stem from the frightened child within.

A good leader
never slanders,
shames, or shuns.

A good leader
does not spread misinformation or pick fights
on Twitter.

A good leader
is not boastful;
their history speaks for itself.

A good leader
knows how to communicate
their soul.

A good leader
knows the United States of America
is a collaborative poem.

A good leader
provides disparate voices a platform
rather than stifling them.

A good leader
asks questions,
and then listens.

But a good leader
is not a puppet
of public opinion
or corporate interests.

A good leader
never pulls your strings
unseen.

A good leader
embodies the words
they speak.

A good leader
constantly questions the goodness
of their leadership.

A good leader
admits their failures
each and every day.

A good leader
strives for a world
without any need for leaders.

A good leader
has nothing to do with
being religious.

A good leader
is well read,
but not necessarily well educated.

A good leader
is more philosophical
than political.

A good leader
is not simply the candidate
who shares your same gang colors.

A good leader
does not care if you think the same as him or her,
so long as you think.

A good leader
is kind and patient and forgiving,
with a good sense of humor.

A good leader
knows how to lose with pride
and win with humility.

A good leader
suffers stoically
without expecting you should do the same.

Everyone who reads this
should strive to be a good leader.

A good leader
tries to make the load a little lighter
for the next leader.

A good leader
knows the end never really justifies the means,
and the means never really justifies the end.

A good leader
never strikes
first.

A good leader won't lay down their life for you,
nor will they ask you
to lay down yours for them.

A good leader
translates complex issues into relatable experiences,
not anger and fear of *the other*.

Nowadays, Charlie Manson's disciples
would have all been
members of congress.

She asked if I believe
aliens had made contact with us.
I said, "Why would an advanced extraterrestrial
civilization ever want to deal with humans
and their inexhaustible drama?"

Maybe it's better to have no leader
than a bad one.

00020

Your friends & family are a prison.

Your school is a prison.

Your job is a prison.

Your house is a prison.

Your spouse is a prison.

Your country is a prison.

Your mind is a prison.

But this world is a wondrous paradise.

Do you think of this universe as a prison?

Do you think of your body as a prison?

Maybe this is where the problem begins…

00021

This flesh is not imprisoned in time.

This flesh is time itself,

and all of space is our desire.

00022

Putting two or more people in a small prison cell
will magnify every irritant a hundredfold—
every little word misspoken,
every little deed misdone,
every askance look.

00023

Simple logic:

A person will never learn how to socialize

in solitary confinement.

00024

Q: Why is evil so fuckin' cool?

A: Because none of us want to get hurt.

Q: How do you deal with people

who knowingly embrace evil?

How do you deal with incorrigibles?

How do you deal with the traumatized,

the abused,

the brainwashed,

the countless souls who've given up hope?

A: Give them hope.

Give them a reason

(a real one)

to believe.

Q: But what do you do with psychopaths?

A: You do what you would do with anyone else

who is suffering from a severe ailment:

You hospitalize them.

You care for them as best you can,

keeping them and others from harm

while trying to heal their psychic wounds.

00025

Everyone in prison needs therapy

more than my well-to-do neighbors.

00026

You're being too soft on 'em.

Prisoners are supposed to feel

like they're being punished.

Scared straight and all.

I say hurt 'em.

Hurt 'em real bad.

Torture 'em.

Whip 'em.

Rape 'em.

Castrate 'em.

That'll put the fear in 'em.

That'll make 'em good.

And if that don't work,

ship 'em off to Murder Island.

Let 'em go play with others of their kind.

We could televise it and everything.

The ratings would go through the roof!

(Didn't they make a movie about that?)

Or remove the part of their brain
that makes 'em bad.
Just keep slicing away until all that's left
is the good stuff.
Of course, we could save everyone the headache
and just execute 'em.
Kill 'em all,
but do it humanely.
It isn't murder if they're murderers.
The law says so.

00027

Getting rid of the cancer

is not the same as

curing the sickness.

Capital punishment

may seem like an enticing way to deal with

the worst of society's unrepentant evildoers,

but in the spirit of the body politic,

wouldn't it be safer to use therapeutic techniques

to regenerate the cancerous cell,

rather than excise it?

What if the cancer is benign?

Cancer is an indication

of the environment's unhealthiness,

not just the body's.

00028

Every prisoner must be taught a trade
or earn a college degree
in the discipline
of their choosing.

Every prisoner must also learn karate,
not to better express their violence,
but to overcome the fear
at the root of it.

Serving in the military
would cut a prisoner's sentence
in half.

Like it or not,
one way or the other,
prisons are reeducation facilities.

The cure is in the curriculum.

00029

Reward prisoners for every book they read.

Books up to approximately 400 pages in length
equal one week off their sentence,
but they must write a two-page, double-spaced
(approximately 500 words)
critical exploration of the work.

Books that are longer than 500 pages
equal one month off their sentence,
provided they write a five-page, double-spaced
(approximately 1,250 words)
critical exploration of the work.

Tutors are available Monday through Friday
from 10:00 a.m. to 5:00 p.m.

00030

Reward prisoners for poems they write.
Reward them with snacks and smokes.
Hold poetry slams in the slammer.
Fight it out with wisdom & jokes.

Cutting remarks,
brutal jabs of insight,
may the sharpest tongue win.

What if prisons taught prisoners to be poets
instead of instilling gang mentality and racism,
freeing their voices
instead of caging their minds?

00031

Virtual reality simulators
could allow violent offenders
to experience firsthand
the harm they do
from the standpoint of the victim.
This would impart a higher level of empathy
for victims of unwarranted violence,
making the prisoner less likely
to commit the same crime
in the future.
Brutality is commensurate
with a lack of empathy.

More money should be spent
on rehabilitative technology
than weapons and means
of subjugation.

Stop declaring war on your own citizens.

00032

Being the strongest or the smartest

or the rightest

won't save humanity

from worldwide annihilation.

Empathy is no guarantee

against extinction,

but at least it gives us

a fighting chance.

00033

Prisoners should be called
those whom society has failed,
and prisons should be called
failures of society.

00034

Free the prisoners.

Prisons should feel more like
high schools and colleges,
and less like
cages in a zoo.

Prisons themselves should be referred to as
rehabilitative housing units.
Incarceration facilities should be converted
into five-bedroom apartments,
rather than cramped cells.

Prisoners themselves should simply be referred to as
health risks
and given grades ranging from one to ten,
as in: "This rehabilitative housing unit
currently houses three level six health risks."

The higher the level,

the more unstable and dangerous

the health risk is

to oneself, others, and society in general.

But imprisonment never comes into play;

health risks are *almost always* reintroduced

into some aspect of society ASAP,

albeit with certain freedoms restricted,

like the right to bear arms, for instance,

or use certain drugs.

Level six health risks

and above

must wear a monitoring device

at all times.

Level ten health risks

must wear a remote-controlled stun collar.

For safety purposes,

all health risks would be housed

with others who share their level,

and a resident advisor one level lower.

Resident advisors must serve their housemates

for one year

before graduating

to the next lower level of health risk.

The rehabilitative housing unit for ninth level health

risks would be overseen by a level eight health risk.

The rehabilitative housing unit for eighth level

health risks would be overseen by a level seven

health risk. The rehabilitative housing unit for

seventh level health risks would be overseen by a

level six health risk, and so on. Appointment to

oversee a rehabilitative housing unit is by

nomination from a lower-level health risk. Due to

the volatile nature of tenth level health risks, their

care is only given to level one health risks, those
who've progressed to enlightened masters of their
will and desires, constituting the final step in their
rehabilitation process.

The lower your health risk,
The more freedom you have.
The more freedom you have,
the more motivated you are
to be free
of health risks.

Citizens with clean records
are deemed non-health risks,
a.k.a. potential health risks.

00035

Citizens with clean records
are never trusted
with the care of health risks.

Only health risks are qualified
to mentor other health risks,
having more empathy than anyone else
for those they once were.

The enlightened correctional system
is based on healthy peer pressure,
positive reinforcement,
and self-policing;
health risks call this self-mastery.

Thus,
those who have furthest fallen
often end up rising
to the highest positions of leadership,
and rightly so,
much to Harvard's chagrin.

00036

A society without jails
wouldn't need jail terms.

No prison sentences.

But this means you could potentially be deemed
a health risk
for the rest of your life.

00037

Citizens can check themselves into
rehabilitative housing units,
just like they would a rehab.

Health risks receive free counseling
and government assistance
to find and secure
housing and employment.

Some health risks choose
to live in rehabilitative housing units
their entire lives.

00038

Any health risk may request

government-funded LSD or MDMA therapy

to overcome addiction

or behavioral issues.

In fact,

it's strongly encouraged.

00039

All drugs must be legal,

easily available,

and inexpensive.

Coupled with an existence wage,

this would eliminate most of society's crime.

00040

Prostitution must be legalized
and sex work unionized.

Sex,
drugs,
music,
literature,
and (consensual) pornography
should never be censored or outlawed.

Outlawing human nature is the surest way
to imprison the world.

00041

Every one of us is guilty.
We've all broken the law
at one time or another
and gotten away with it.
We've all aided and abetted
in one way or another,
harboring the criminal within.

Let him who is without sin cast the first stone…

00042

As long as humans are involved,

there will be corruption, ineptitude, and injustice.

Human error must be removed from the equation

of justice

without losing what makes us human.

Computers make errors as well,

but at least they're honest errors.

In the near future,

artificial intelligence will be capable of

calculating a quadrillion algorithms

of context and legal parameters of behavior

per second,

dispensing justice

on a more objective and personalized level.

Q: But what about all those movies

where A.I. tries to take over the world

by wiping out the humans?

A: I suggest you consider all those *other* movies

(of which there are a thousand times more)

where *humans* try to take over the world

by wiping out their fellow humans.

00043

What if
there were no me
and there were no you,
only both of us connected
intimately
through and through?

How could I willfully harm you
or you harm me
if our minds were conjoined
virtually?

Group-mind,
hive-mind,
no mind as we now know it.
Maybe no mind at all.
Let the sci-fi writers speculate
while the naysayers verbally feculate.
Hyper-social media is an evolutionary response
to the deadly future's call.

00044

Be careful not to cure the humans

of their humanness.

00045

I hear your tired arguments:
If we give the addicts free money and drugs,
they'll sit around all day
playing video games and watching Netflix.

At least they won't be out there
committing crimes
to afford their habit.

But making drugs legal and affordable
will encourage addiction.

The cost and illegality of a drug
never kept any of my friends
from becoming addicted.

But I shouldn't have to pay taxes

for them to be slackers.

As of 2022,

U.S. law enforcement and the prison system

cost taxpayers

over $35 billion annually.

But where will all this "free" money come from?

There were approximately six million

unemployed U.S. adults in 2022.

6,000,000 multiplied by

$30,000 (a modest annual existence wage)

= 180 billion dollars.

The U.S. defense budget for 2022

was over 770 billion dollars.

What if we had used some of that defense money

to defend the well-being of our citizens

on the home front?

Would it really have been the end of the world
if our annual defense budget only totaled
590 billion dollars?

Heck, we should've just made it an even 500 billion
and used the other 90 billion to help raise everyone
who's fallen below the poverty line.

$500,000,000,000 is more than enough for defense.
America already has 3,708 active nuclear warheads.
Scientists have concluded it would only take 100
to fuck the world completely.

If you find these ideas naive,
I invite you to come up with something better.

00046

For the poesy police who gripe
about too much prose in these poems,
remember The Three Artopian Rules:

My body,
my choice.

My mind,
my choice.

My self-expression,
my choice.

But please feel free to keep looking
for trifling ways
to persecute your fellow human.

This poem isn't about poetry.
Over-policing comes in many guises.

Free the verse!

00047

The cornerstone of Artopian architecture:

Nature is the reflection we perceive
of the universal mind.
The universal mind is psychedelic.
Consider the flowers and the seashells
and the electromagnetic wavelength.

All matter is a psychoactive substance.
Nature is hallucinatory,
thinking in fractals,
just like us.

The more our architecture comes to emulate and
incorporate living nature
(and not the cold, precise angles
of humanmade logic
constructed with dead and deadly materials),
the healthier we'll be,
mentally and physically
and spiritually.

00048

The universe,

the stars,

the formation of life,

the complexity of our brains—

everything's miraculous.

It's all one big miracle

we take for granted

every second of the day.

00049

It's only a poem
hastily written
before the numbness creeps back,
and I wish it were better,
stronger,
healthier,
wiser,
kinder,
more patient,
more forgiving.

I wish it could take all your pain
and turn it to inspiration.

I wish it could take all your doubt
and turn it to hope.

But it's only a poem.

And I am just a poet
in a world of mad god-kings.

J. Martin Strangeweather and a police officer walk into a crowded pizza parlor in downtown Santa Ana at approximately ten o' clock on a Friday night. While waiting in line to order, Strangeweather strikes up a conversation with the police officer.

"So, do you live in Santa Ana?"

"I don't feel comfortable telling you where I live, sir." The police officer immediately goes on the defensive, as anyone would when feeling threatened.

"Sure, I understand," says Strangeweather. "It's just that cops who don't live in the community they serve tend to care less about serving it humanely."

"Is there anything else you'd like to ask me, sir?"

"You betcha," says Strangeweather, five beers deep into a night of barhopping, feeling dangerously courageous. "Do you think prisons work?"

"What do you mean by *work?*"

"Do you think prisons rehabilitate prisoners?"

"No comment."

"What could be done to lower the percentage of recidivism?"

"I'm afraid I can't answer questions like that. It's above my paygrade, sir."

"But surely you must have some thoughts on the matter?"

"I just get paid to do my job, not to think about it."

The police officer depicted here is a one-dimensional character, poorly written… yet he's real. This event really happened. Here's what I said to the police officer on my way out the door, towing two giant slices of pepperoni pizza in a to-go box: "I'm not your enemy, bud. If you look at me and see anything but a fellow American—*a fellow human*—you're part of the problem."

I could feel the sting of hypocrisy as the words left my mouth.

J. Martin Strangeweather believes three left turns will set you on the right path. He served nineteen consecutive life sentences in the imprisoned mind before escaping down a rabbit hole to a secret wonderland he dubbed the Strangeverse. Strangeweather has since become one of the world's foremost rabbit hole spelunkers. You can find more of his explorations at: www.jmartinstrangeweather.com